Crabapples

Dirt Movers

Bobbie Kalman & Petrina Gentile

 Crabtree Publishing Company

Crabapples

created by Bobbie Kalman

for Danielle Gentile

Editor-in-Chief
Bobbie Kalman

Writing team
Bobbie Kalman
Petrina Gentile

Managing editor
Lynda Hale

Editors
Tammy Everts
David Schimpky

Computer design
Lynda Hale
David Schimpky

Color separations and film
Dot 'n Line Image Inc.

Printer
Worzalla Publishing Company

Special thanks to
Ed Lamb, Les Hildebrand, and John Lemieux of Walker Brothers Quarries Ltd.; Danielle Gentile (the model who appears on the covers and throughout the book); Bob Sobota Construction; Hard Rock Paving; Hugh Cole Construction; Philip Environmental; Red-D-Mix Concrete; Sam Adelstein & Company Ltd.; and Steed & Evans Ltd.

Illustrations
David Carson: pages 5, 7, 10, 12, 13, 14, 16, 18, 22, 23, 24-25, 28, 30-31
Tammy Everts: pages 6, 9, 11, 15, 17, 20-21, 26

Photographs
Marc Crabtree: pages 26, 28
Bobbie Kalman: page 5
Diane Payton Majumdar: front and back covers, title page, pages 4, 6, 7, 8-9, 10, 11, 12, 13 (both), 14, 15, 16 (both), 18, 19, 21, 22, 23, 27 (both), 29 (both), 32

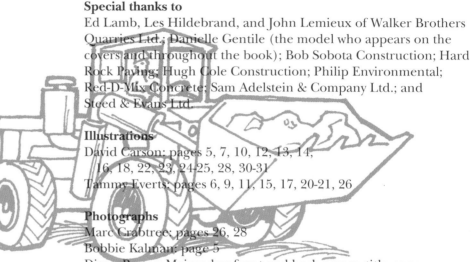

Crabtree Publishing Company

350 Fifth Avenue	360 York Road, RR 4	73 Lime Walk
Suite 3308	Niagara-on-the-Lake	Headington
New York	Ontario, Canada	Oxford OX3 7AD
N.Y. 10118	L0S 1J0	United Kingdom

Cataloging in Publication Data
Kalman, Bobbie, 1947-
   Dirt movers

(Crabapples)
Includes index.

ISBN 0-86505-607-2 (library bound)   ISBN 0-86505-707-9 (pbk.)
Dump trucks, backhoes, bulldozers, and cranes are among the construction vehicles discussed in this book.

1. Construction equipment - Juvenile literature. 2. Earthmoving machinery - Juvenile literature. I. Gentile, Petrina, 1969-   .
II. Title. III. Series: Kalman, Bobbie, 1947-   . Crabapples.

TH900.K35 1994   j624.028   LC 94-34783
                                                       CIP

What is in this book?

What is a dirt mover?

A dirt mover is a machine. Some dirt movers dig into the ground. Others move dirt, snow, and rock.

Some dirt movers pick up garbage. Some are used to build roads or houses.

Wheels and crawlers

treads

Some dirt movers have giant wheels. Giant wheels have big rubber **treads**. A tread is the part of the wheel that touches the ground. Giant wheels can ride over bumpy ground.

Some dirt movers move on **crawlers**. Crawlers have steel treads. Steel treads can move over bumps more smoothly than tires can.

Crawlers can climb up steep banks. The treads grip the ground. The wide bottom stops the machine from sinking into soft dirt or mud.

Dirt mover parts

Dirt movers have many parts. Some parts move. Others do not. The drawing on the next page shows how the parts of a dirt mover work together to grab dirt.

The driver sits in the **cab**. It has glass all around so the driver can see everything. The cab is soundproof.

Some dirt movers are so big that the driver has to use a ladder to climb up to the cab.

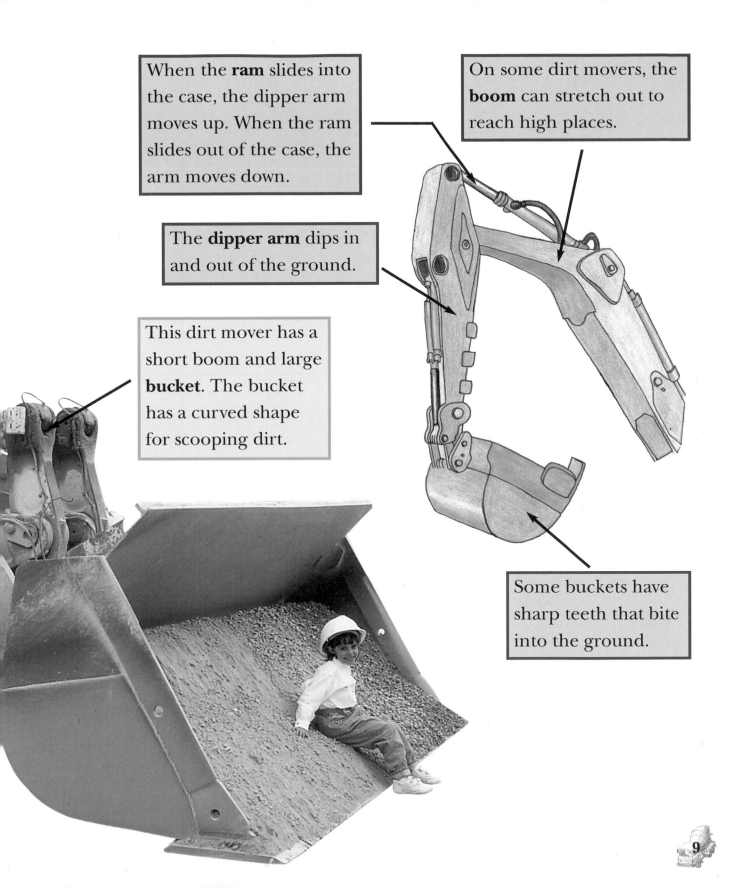

When the **ram** slides into the case, the dipper arm moves up. When the ram slides out of the case, the arm moves down.

On some dirt movers, the **boom** can stretch out to reach high places.

The **dipper arm** dips in and out of the ground.

This dirt mover has a short boom and large **bucket**. The bucket has a curved shape for scooping dirt.

Some buckets have sharp teeth that bite into the ground.

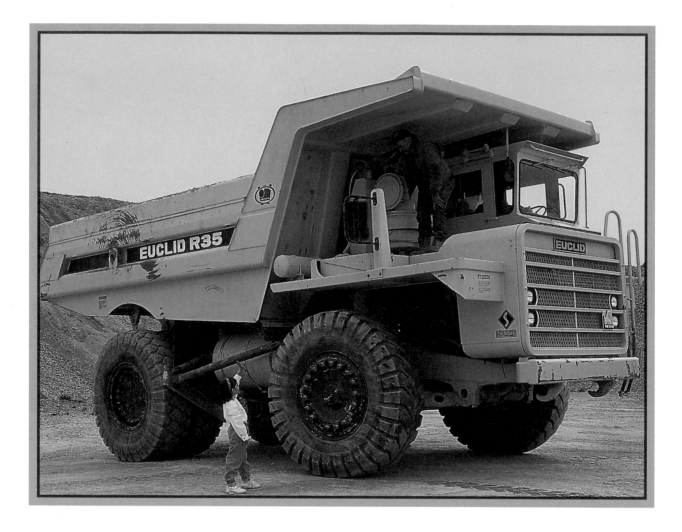

Giant dumpers

Giant dump trucks can move lots of dirt. They can carry heavy rocks. Some are five times as tall as a child. Measure this dump truck to see how many times higher it is than Danielle.

Some dump trucks have a **tilting** dumper. The body tilts from side to side to keep the heavy load in place.

The dump truck below has a **V-shaped dumper**. The V shape of the dumper stops the load from moving around in the truck.

tilting dumper

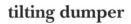

11

Working together

A dump truck can carry a load, but it cannot load itself. It needs help from a front-end loader. The loader digs the dirt, scoops it with its big scoop, and lifts it up to the truck.

The loader must dig, scoop, lift, and dump many times to fill the truck. When the truck is full, the driver drives it away.

To empty the truck, the driver tilts up the dumper. The back opens, and the dirt comes spilling down!

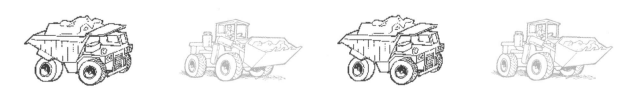

Dozing the ground

Bulldozers **doze** the ground. Dozing the ground means clearing the dirt, stones, or sand out of the way.

Bulldozers have a big steel blade. The blade is not flat. It is curved. The curved shape scoops the dirt as it pushes it away.

Sometimes there is a big spike at the back of a bulldozer. The spike is called a **ripper**. The ripper drags behind the bulldozer. It breaks up hard ground.

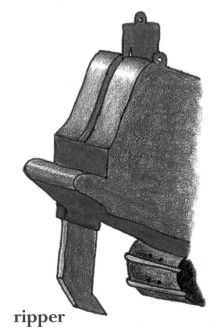

ripper

Dirt diggers

Excavators are digging machines. They dig, lift, load, doze, and dump dirt!

A backhoe can dig deep pits. It has a bucket with sharp teeth.

Sometimes there is an **auger** on the excavator. An auger has very sharp edges! It can drill deep holes.

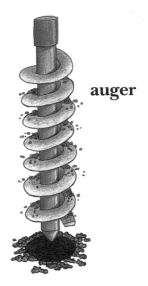

auger

A dragline excavator can dig giant holes. It has cables called **draglines**. The draglines pull a huge bucket through the dirt. The bucket is so big that a car can fit inside it!

dragline

Mixing and pouring

drum

delivery chute

Concrete is made from sand, gravel, cement, and water. It is made in the **drum** of a concrete mixer. The drum has blades inside for mixing.

When the drum turns one way, the blades mix the concrete. When it turns the other way, the concrete pours out of the **delivery chute**.

Making a road

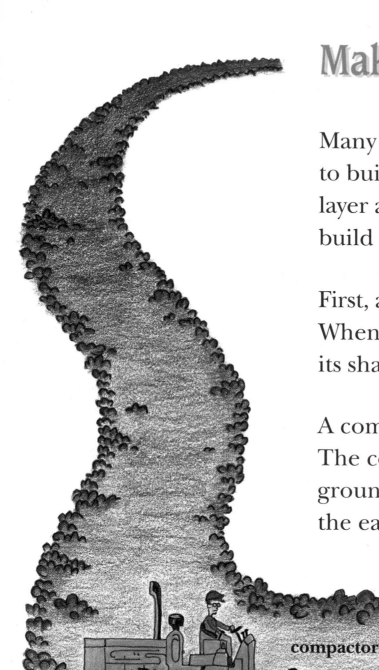

Many kinds of dirt movers are used to build roads. Roads are made one layer at a time. It takes a long time to build up the many layers of a road.

First, a scraper smoothes the ground. When the machine moves forward, its sharp blade scrapes the dirt.

A compactor follows the scraper. The compactor drives over the ground many times. It flattens the earth with its heavy wheels.

compactor

scraper

A grader follows the compactor.
It has a huge steel blade. The blade
spreads a layer of small stones over
the ground. The stones become
the bottom layer of the road.

Paving a road

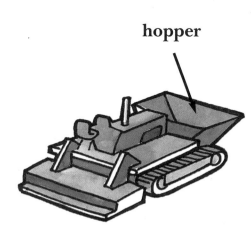

hopper

Roads are paved with **asphalt**. Asphalt is a mixture of hot tar and tiny stones. A dump truck pours asphalt into the **hopper** of the paver. The hopper is at the front.

The metal blade of the paver spreads the hot asphalt on the ground. The asphalt gets hard as it cools.

Some rollers are big. Some rollers are small. Some can be pushed by hand. A roller flattens asphalt by rolling over it. Rollers drive back and forth over the asphalt until the road is hard and strong.

The metal wheels of rollers are hollow inside. Sometimes they are filled with water or sand. Water and sand make the wheels even heavier.

A rock quarry

A **quarry** is an open pit filled with rocks. Rocks are used to make roads and buildings. They are dug out of the quarry. Sometimes they are blasted out with dynamite.

rock breaker

The rock breaker on the opposite
page breaks big chunks of rock into
small pieces! Front-end loaders load
the rocks into dump trucks. The
dump trucks carry the rocks away.

Pushers and cleaners

Snowplows clear snow from roads. Some snowplows have one blade at the front. The blade is slanted left or right. It pushes the snow to the side of the road. Some snowplows have two blades. They can clear a wide path through the snow.

A garbage truck picks up garbage. It squeezes it together so that lots of garbage will fit inside.

The truck takes the garbage to a **landfill site**. At the landfill site, the garbage is covered with dirt and more garbage.

Big cranes

Cranes are used to move very heavy objects. They have hooks, buckets, or magnets for lifting. **Pulleys** help cranes lift and move loads. A pulley is a wheel with a cable around it.

pulley

pulley

The crane on the left is on the back of a truck. It is called a truck crane. It moves on wheels.

The crawler cranes below move on crawler tracks. The crane and cab can spin around on the tracks.

Crawler cranes can move only on flat ground. If the ground is too bumpy—watch out—the crane could tip over!

Picture glossary & Index

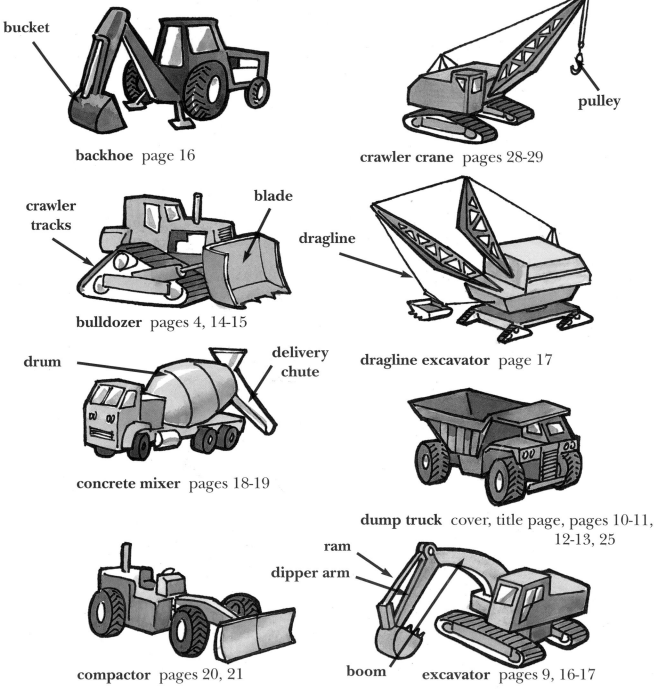

bucket

backhoe page 16

pulley

crawler crane pages 28-29

crawler tracks

blade

bulldozer pages 4, 14-15

dragline

dragline excavator page 17

drum

delivery chute

concrete mixer pages 18-19

dump truck cover, title page, pages 10-11, 12-13, 25

ram

dipper arm

compactor pages 20, 21

boom

excavator pages 9, 16-17

loader

bucket

front-end loader pages 8-9, 12-13, 25, back cover

rod

rock breaker pages 24-25

garbage truck page 27

roller page 23

blade

grader page 21

blade

scraper page 20

hopper

paver page 22

blade

snow plow page 26

Dirt movers are everywhere!

The next time you are in a car, count
and name the dirt movers you see.

If you can name:
- more than 15, you are a TOWER CRANE!
- from 13-15, you are a BIG WHEEL.
- between 10-12, you are a ROLLER.
- as many as 7-9, you are a LOADER.
- as few as 4-6, you are DOZING around!
- only 1-3, you are a CRAWLER!

5 6 7 8 9 0 Printed in USA 3 2 1 0 9